FORTY STEPS
CLOSER TO GOD

FORTY STEPS
CLOSER TO GOD

*A Book of 40 Hadith With Commentary
for Young Muslim Adults*

Bushra Bajwa

For Fehsal, Maheen and Sabeen

CONTENTS

FOREWORD

In the Quran, God tells Muslims that, "Verily you have in the Prophet of Allah an excellent model for him who fears Allah and the Last Day and who remembers Allah much" (33:22). Since Prophet Muhammad^{sas} was divinely appointed a perfect example for humankind, it was necessary, that a detailed record of his words and deeds should be preserved for the benefit of later generations.

What the Holy Prophet^{sas} said and did has been compiled into a collection known as hadith, or traditions. These began to be collected shortly after his demise. The compilers of hadith carefully tested the accuracy and reliability of each narrator in the chain of transmission of a hadith. If a single narrator in the chain of communication was of doubtful integrity, or authenticity, in respect to memory, intelligence or character, his testimony was rejected, and the hadith was discarded. Also, each hadith must conform with the Holy Quran. The Holy Prophet[sas] admonished that nothing could be accredited to him which was in any way in conflict with the Holy Quran.

There are six principal collections of hadith which are regarded by the main body of Orthodox Islam as authentic, namely, the compilations of Imams Bukhari, Muslim, Al-Tirmidhi, Ibne Maja, Abu Dawud, and An-Nasai. Some others, for instance, the Muatta of Imam Malik, and the Musnad of Imam Ahmad bin Hanbal rank almost as high. There are many others of varying degrees of authenticity.

To serve as the perfect example for humankind the Holy Prophet's[sas] life was bound to be multi-faceted. During the Holy Prophet's[sas] mere 23 years as a prophet, he faced many different roles, responsibilities, and challenges. It was necessary that a complete picture of his way of life and of what he taught, should be readily available for his followers. The narrators and compilers of hadith have filled this need, to whom Muslims, and all those interested in upholding moral and spiritual values, owe a debt of gratitude.

In this book, a humble effort has been made to present the mode of life of the Holy Prophet[sas]. The selected forty hadith were chosen to provide both examples of Prophet Muhammad's[sas] relationship with God as well as his relationship with his fellow beings. They are presented in this book in no particular order. Adopting the habits demonstrated in these forty hadith would not only bring one closer to God but would also lead to more peaceful societies. I hope these select hadith prove useful for Muslim youth and young adults as they try to adopt the wise ways of our Perfect Leader.

Explanatory notes:

1. The letters ^{sas} are added each time after stating the name of the Holy Prophet Muhammad^{sas}. These letters are an abbreviation for 'Sallallahu-alaihe-wasalam' which means, 'May peace and blessings of Allah be upon him.'

2. The letters ^{ra} are added after the name of any Disciple of the Prophet^{sas}. These letters are an abbreviation for 'Radi Allahu 'anhu/'anha/'anhum' which means 'May Allah be pleased with him/with her/with them.'

3. The word 'he' applies to both male and female believers.

4. The Holy Prophet^{sas} often used the expression 'brother' as meaning a fellow Muslim or fellow human being.

5. Each of the 40 hadith is written in bold at the top of the page, followed by a commentary of the hadith. Additional hadith have been added to the explanation to further elaborate on the topic.

6. Two discussion questions are provided at the end of each topic to test the reader's understanding of the subject. Some questions may require further thought on the topic. These questions make this an ideal book for a book club or a religious study group.

Forty Steps Closer To God

WORSHIP OF GOD DURING ONE'S YOUTH

Abu Hurairah[ra] narrates that the Holy Prophet[sas] said, 'There are seven whom Allah will shade on the Day of Judgement... [of these the second is] the man who devotes his life to the worship of God even in his youth' (*Bukhari* and *Muslim*).

Youth is generally a time when one has energy and enjoys good health. We should take advantage of this period to spend more time and effort engaged in worship and carrying out other good deeds as these tasks may get more difficult with age. Prophet Muhammad[sas] advised, 'Take advantage of five things before five things take place: take advantage of your youth before you grow old. Take advantage of your free time before you become busy.

Take advantage of your life before your death. Take advantage of your health before you become sick. And take advantage of your richness before you become poor' (*Al-Tirmidhi*).

During our adolescent years, we have to make some crucial decisions which shape our future. These can impact the path of our spiritual journeys and affect our lives. One who is already engaged in the worship of God at this time will benefit from making decisions that will help him to continue on the right path.

Youth is also a time when one is faced by many desires. If one can control and overcome these Satanic attacks and follow the path of God, then he or she has paved the way for a better future for him or herself. The Prophet[sas] said to Ibn Abbaas[ra] when he was a young boy, 'Be mindful of Allah and He will take care of you. Whoever engages in good works and worship in their youth, Allah will protect him when he gets older' (*Al-Tirmidhi*).

Questions:

1. What is the advantage of worshiping God during one's youth?

2. How do our actions during our youth impact our future life?

REMEMBRANCE OF ALLAH

Abu Hurairah[ra] relates that the Holy Prophet[sas] said, 'There are two phrases that are easy on the tongue, but are heavy on the scales, and are loved by the Gracious One:

سبحان الله وبحمده، سبحان الله العظيم

Exalted is Allah with all His Glory, Exalted is Allah with all His Majesty' (**Bukhari** and **Muslim**).

Remembrance of Allah refers to the different ways of remembering Allah. That is, thinking about His attributes, reciting them regularly, believing in them sincerely, and reflecting upon His Omnipotence and Power.

Remembrance of Allah is higher in status than all other acts of worship. Abu Dardaa[ra] relates that when the Holy Prophet[sas] addressed his companions, he said,

'Shall I tell you about your best action and the noblest deed (even for the kings) which raises your status, and is better for you than spending gold and silver?' The companions said, 'Certainly, please tell us.' The Holy Prophet^{sas} said, 'It is the Remembrance of Allah' (*Al-Tirmidhi*).

Regularly being occupied in the Remembrance of Allah is a way to show sincere gratitude to God for His endless bounties. The Holy Prophet^{sas} said when people gather together for the Remembrance of Allah they are surrounded by angels and are covered by mercy from their Lord. The more time we spend remembering Allah, the more we attract the company of angels. This is beneficial for us because angels continuously remind us to perform good deeds.

Remembrance of Allah enhances our love for God and brings us closer to Him. The Holy Prophet^{sas} made the comparison between a person who remembers his Lord and a person who does not, equal to the comparison between the living and the dead. That is, he who remembers Allah is spiritually alive and he, who does not, is spiritually dead. This clearly shows the importance of the Remembrance of Allah.

Questions:

1. In what ways can we engage in the Remembrance of Allah?
2. What is the benefit of engaging in the Remembrance of Allah?

INVOKE BLESSINGS ON THE HOLY PROPHET^{SAS}

Ibn Mas'ud^{ra} relates that the Holy Prophet^{sas} said, 'The closest to me on the Day of Judgment will be those who call down blessings on me most' (*Al-Tirmidhi*).

اللَّهُمَّ صَلِّ عَلَى مُحَمَّدٍ وَعَلَى آلِ مُحَمَّدٍ كَمَا صَلَّيْتَ

عَلَى إِبْرَاهِيمَ وَعَلَى آلِ إِبْرَاهِيمَ إِنَّكَ حَمِيدٌ مَجِيدٌ

اللَّهُمَّ بَارِكْ عَلَى مُحَمَّدٍ وَ عَلَى آلِ مُحَمَّدٍ كَمَا بَارَكْتَ عَلَى

إِبْرَاهِيمَ وَ عَلَى آلِ إِبْرَاهِيمَ إِنَّكَ حَمِيدٌ مَجِيدٌ

O Allah, Bless Muhammad^{sas} and the people of Muhammad^{sas} as You did bless Abraham^{as} and the people of Abraham^{as}. You are indeed the Praiseworthy, the Glorious.

O Allah, Prosper Muhammad^{sas} and the people of Muhammad^{sas} as You did prosper

*Abraham*as *and the people of Abraham*as*. You
are indeed the Praiseworthy, the Glorious.*

The practice of invoking *durood* is an opportunity given
by God to true believers to gain merit for themselves.
Since God's favors on the Holy Prophetsas are bound-
less, anyone who invokes *durood* on him, owing to personal love, gets a measure of the tremendous blessings
also. That is because, a person who seeks blessings for
another, due to personal love, becomes a part of them.
Thus, the beneficence granted to the person for whom
blessings are sought is also awarded to the person seek-
ing blessings.

Once a man came in the presence of the Holy
Prophetsas and offered *salaat* and then prayed, 'O God
forgive me and have mercy on me.' The Holy Prophetsas
said to him that he had been a little hasty. For the acceptance of prayers, he should have first glorified and praised

God, then invoked *durood* on the Prophet[sas] and then supplicated to God.

The Holy Prophet[sas] also said when you listen to the voice of the *muezzin* calling for prayer, repeat his words and then invoke *durood*. The person who invokes Durood has ten-fold blessings from God.

The Holy Prophet[sas] also counseled his followers to 'Profusely invoke *durood* on me on Friday for this is the day your invocation of *durood* will be presented to me' (*Abu Dawud*). Thus, believers should recite the *durood* even more profusely on Fridays to partake in this blessing.

Durood should be recited abundantly. It should not be recited as a ritual or in a parrot-like fashion, but while keeping in view the grace and bounties of the Holy Prophet[sas]. We should recite *durood* to elevate the station of Prophet Muhammad[sas], for his success, and for the acceptance of our prayers.

Questions:

1. Why should we invoke *durood* on the Holy Prophet[sas]?

2. How should *durood* be recited?

RECITATION OF THE QURAN

Abu Umamah[ra] relates that he heard the Holy Prophet[sas] say, 'Keep reading the Quran for it will intercede for its readers on the Day of Judgment' (*Muslim*).

The Holy Quran is a perfect and complete book sent by God for all people, for all times to come. It remains in its original form to this day as Allah has been safeguarding every word of the Holy Quran since the day of its revelation and will continue to do so.

The recitation of the Quran purifies the heart and helps get rid of spiritual and moral weaknesses. We should try to make it a habit to recite the Quran every day, read its translation and reflect on it. The real objective of reciting the Holy Quran is to be informed of its truths and knowledge so that we can bring about a positive change in ourselves. By reading the Quran regularly, we can better understand it and follow its teachings. It also demonstrates our love for God and our desire to draw nearer to Him. Thus, the Quran should be read regularly, carefully and with concentration.

Abu Hurairah[ra] relates that he heard the Holy Prophet[sas] say, 'Allah does not lend an ear so joyously to anything as he does to the recitation of the Quran by a Prophet who has a beautiful voice and recites well and audibly' (*Bukhari* and *Muslim*). Also, reciting the Quran with a beautiful voice, beautifies the Quran and enhances our love for it. Thus, the melodious recitation of the Quran is particularly pleasing to Allah.

Questions:

1. How can we ensure that we obey the commandments of God?

2. Why should the Quran be recited in a melodious voice?

COMPASSION AND FORGIVENESS

Habbar Bin Aswad attacked the Holy Prophet's[sas] daughter, Zainab[ra], as she tried to flee from Mecca to Medina. Zainab[ra], who was pregnant, fell off her camel. She sustained injuries, including the termination of her pregnancy and later died from the injuries she suffered from this fall. When the Muslims, some years later, conquered Mecca, Habbar Bin Aswad was sentenced to death. He fled out of fear of his life. But when he learned about the compassion and forgiveness of the Holy Prophet[sas], he went to visit him and begged for his mercy. He said, 'I ran away for your fear, but your forgiveness and mercy have brought me back. O Prophet of God! We were ignorant and idol worshippers. Through you, God saved us from death; I feel guilty of my excesses, forgive me, ignoring my ignorance.' The Holy Prophet^sas forgave this murderer of his daughter and said, 'Go Habbar, I have forgiven you, this is Allah's favor on you that you accepted Islam.'

The Prophet^sas, whom Allah has called, 'The Compassionate' and 'The Merciful' had very tender feelings for his followers, as well as humankind in general, including his enemies. It was because of his intense love for Allah that he loved all of God's creatures and could forgive even his most bitter enemies.

The Holy Prophet^sas and his companions had to bear extreme pain and suffering at the hands of their enemies. Women's legs would be tied to two camels that would be made to run in opposite directions thereby tearing apart their bodies. At one point, the Muslims were isolated in a desolate valley, She'eb Abi Talib, for two and a half years. Even then, Prophet Muhammad[sas] wished well for his enemies. Instead of having any feelings of anger or hatred towards the disbelievers, the Prophet[sas] felt great anguish for them and prayed to Allah to save their future generations. His perfect character of mercy and kindness towards others is the most excellent model for all of humankind.

In Taif, he faced the worst torment and torture of his life. He said, 'The worst day of my agony was when I went to the chief of Taif' (*Bukhari* and *Muslim*). Prophet Muhammad's[sas] followers requested him to pray against the troublemakers of Taif and God sent an angel to inform the Prophet[sas] of the impending destruction of the people of Taif, only waiting upon the Holy Prophet's[sas] very say so. Yet the Prophet[sas] prayed for the guidance of the people of Taif. He advised his followers to be patient and taught them that real recompense was not in praying against one's enemies, but by praying for their guidance. His prayers saved the city of Taif from destruction. Even during this incident, in which the Holy Prophet Muhammad^{sas} received the worst pain of his life, he still prayed for the mercy and guidance of his enemies.

At the Conquest of Mecca, which was the victory of Islam, the Prophet^{sas} declared to the Meccans, 'By God, you will have no punishment today and no reproof'(Quran, 12:92). Despite the years of torment and hardship the Prophet^{sas} and his companions faced at the hands of the Meccans, he forgave them in an instance.

A true believer should follow this example and lay the foundation of peace. If someone commits an error, instead of holding a grudge against them or highlighting their mistake, we should try to forgive them, especially if they display a readiness to change. We should show sympathy towards others as we expect them to show it to us, and we should forgive people's mistakes as we hope God will forgive ours.

Questions:

1. Why should we be compassionate towards others?
2. How did the Holy Prophet[sas] save the city of Taif from destruction?

CARE FOR PARENTS

The Holy Prophet^{sas} once recounted an incident, 'Three people, of a people before you, went on a journey when they were overtaken by a storm. They took shelter in a cave. The entrance of the cave was blocked by a huge rock. The travelers decided to beseech God for deliverance by recalling some righteous deed. One of them supplicated, "O Allah my parents were old, and I used to give them food before my wife, children, and servants. Once I came home late, by that time my parents had fallen asleep. I did not consider it appropriate to disturb them nor to feed the rest of my family before them. I brought milk for them and waited that whenever they wake up, I can provide milk to them. The whole night passed in this manner; they woke up in the morning and drank the milk. O my Allah, if I did that deed to seek Your pleasure, then relieve us from this distress and remove this rock." Allah listened to his supplication and the rock moved a little bit.' [After that the other two men related their noblest deeds and prayed for the removal of the rock: Allah granted their prayers and the stone moved entirely from the entrance] (*Bukhari*).

The love, kindness, and care we get from our parents is something that we cannot repay. It is for this reason that we should always respect and love our parents for the sacrifice and attention they gave us when we were children. When parents reach old age and are dependent on others, we should be there to help them and serve them. Once Abdullah-Bin-Masood[ra] asked the Holy Prophet[sas] to tell him the deed most liked by Almighty Allah. The Holy Prophet^{sas} replied that it was to offer prayers on time. He asked him to tell him the second-best deed liked by Allah. The Holy Prophet^{sas} said to him that it was to behave nicely with parents.

In particular, the Holy Prophet^{sas} emphasized love for one's mother. Once a man came to the Prophet^{sas} and asked to whom he should show most kindness, the Prophet^{sas}, replied, 'To your mother.' The man asked who he should show kindness to after his mother. Again, the Prophet^{sas} replied, 'To your mother.' The man asked a third time, and the Prophet^{sas} replied once more, 'Your mother.' Only after he was asked a fourth time, did the Prophet^{sas} respond, 'Your father' (*Bukari* and *Muslim*).

Once a person came to Holy Prophet^{sas} and sought his advice about taking part in Jihad with him. The Holy Prophet^{sas} asked him whether his mother was alive? He answered, yes. The Holy Prophet[sas] then told him to go back home and serve her as Heaven was under her feet.

In addition to parents, the relatives and friends of parents should be treated kindly as well. The Holy Prophet[sas] stressed strengthening the ties of kinship by serving the relatives of parents and treating them with respect and love. He used to say that a father's brother is like a father and that a father's friend should be given the same respect as an uncle. Similarly, a mother's sister has equal standing as a mother and a mother's friend should be respected as mother's sisters.

Service to one's parents and gratitude towards them does not end with their life but continues after their death as well. One should always tread on the path of righteousness so that the reward of our good deeds continues to reach our parents as well. One should also offer prayers for the forgiveness and exalted status of one's parents.

Questions:

1. How can children serve their parents?

2. Who else should be treated with respect and love similar to that of a parent?

PRAYER IN CONGREGATION

Abu Hurairah[ra] relates that the Holy Prophet[sas] said, 'The prayer of a person with the congregation is twenty-five-times more beneficent than his prayer at home. That is because when he performs his ablutions carefully and then proceeds to the mosque for the sole purpose of the prayer, every step that he takes raises his status and wipes out his sins. While he is in his place of prayer in a state of purity the angels keep calling down blessings on him saying: Allah send down blessings on him; Allah, have mercy on him. He is deemed to be occupied in prayer while he waits for it' (*Bukhari* and *Muslim*).

Allah gives more reward to a believer for praying in congregation than for the prayers he or she performs individually. This is because congregational prayer creates equality and unity amongst worshippers. There are specific instructions on how prayers in congregation should be performed. For example, the feet of all worshippers in a row should be aligned, and worshippers should stand shoulder-to-shoulder. These explicit instructions, which require worshippers to pray uniformly, are so that all worshippers turn into one being. Regardless of wealth, family status or color, everyone becomes equal. The aim of praying together is that believers become influenced by each other's good deeds and shun any sense of arrogance or feeling of superiority.

The Holy Prophet[sas] likened prayer in congregation to a frontier. Just like countries establish frontiers on their borders with other countries and appoint armed forces to protect the country from attack, similarly believers can unite to defend themselves from Satanic attacks by praying in congregation. To be protected from the worldly desires that Satan creates in us, congregational prayers serve as a frontier. It is a battalion of guardians that will protect us from such attacks. When unity emerges amongst worshippers and when spirituality advances, then the satanic forces are weakened and diminished. This is the excellence of reading prayers in congregation.

If one is not able to make it to the mosque, then offering one's prayer in congregation at home is better than offering it alone. Children can say their prayers in congregation with their mother and other siblings at home if the father is not present.

Questions:

1. What is the significance of believers praying in congregation?
2. With what did the Holy Prophet[sas] equate congregational prayers?

DISPLAY HUMILITY

Iyad ibn Himar[ra] reports that the Holy Prophet[sas] said that, 'Allah has revealed to me that you should comport yourselves with humility towards one another so that no one transgresses against another, nor boasts of any superiority over another' (*Muslim*).

A person who looks down on others because he thinks of himself as more knowledgeable, wealthy, or higher in status than others is arrogant because he forgets that his wealth, status and dignity were given to him by God and can be taken away from him at any time. By being down-to-earth; meek and humble; and free from all mischief, Muslims can avail of God's mercy and blessings.

The Holy Prophet[sas] was the most exemplary

embodiment of humility despite the grand spiritual status that Allah the Exalted had bestowed on him. He used
to help with the housework, feed and tie the animals,
eat food with his servants, and help them in kneading
dough and bringing rations from the market. Abdullah
bin Abi ʿAwfa[ra] reported that the Holy Prophet[sas] never
hesitated about going with a slave or a widow to accom-
plish his or her tasks. Anas[ra] reported that the Prophet[sas]
used to visit the sick, attend funerals, and accept a poor
man's invitation for a meal.

Prophet Muhammad[sas] taught that one should adopt
humility to such an extent that no-one should feel pride
over another. The Holy Prophet[sas] informed that Allah
would grant one who chooses to forsake fine clothes
only for the sake of humility, regardless of being able to
afford them, the choice to select a 'garment of faith' of
their liking. That is, when one adopts habits of humility,
God bestows him with good qualities. It is these good

qualities that are a believer's 'garments of faith' which enable him to do further good.

Pride and arrogance are barriers to attaining the pleasure of God Almighty, while sincerity and humility are qualities that lead to internal peace, peace between humankind and are pleasing to God. We should remember that our qualities cannot make us worthy of blessings other than with the grace of God and it is the grace of God alone that can adorn our present life and the next life.

Questions:

1. What does an arrogant person forget?
2. In what ways did the Holy Prophet^{sas} display humility?

STRIVE TOWARDS ALLAH

Anas[ra] **relates that the Holy Prophet**[sas] **said, 'Allah says when a servant of Mine advances towards Me a foot, I advance towards him a yard, and when he advances towards Me a yard, I advance towards him the length of his arms spread out. When he comes to Me walking, I go to him running'** (*Bukhari*).

God promises to show the way to one who strives in His way, helping him along the way. When someone sins, they become distant from God. But when he turns to God to repent of his sins, God displays His attributes of mercy and compassion towards him.

Abu Musa Ash'ari[ra] relates that the Holy Prophet[sas] said, 'Allah will continue to hold out His hand at night so that he who has sinned during the day might repent, and to hold out His hand during the day so that he who has sinned at night, might repent, till the sun should rise from the west' (*Muslim*). Allah is always there for us so we should strive in His way to benefit from His forgiveness and receive His blessings. The Holy Prophet[sas] said that, if a person determines upon a virtuous deed but is unable to perform it, Allah records it as one complete righteous deed in his favor. If having determined upon it, he proceeds to perform it as well, it counts with Allah ten-fold or seven hundred-fold or many hundred-fold. On the contrary, if a person conceives of a sinful act but does not commit it, it will count with Allah as one virtuous deed. If he proceeds to commit it, Allah will record it as just one sin. This is the Loving God who is always looking for the good in us, that's why we should strive to do good.

When someone faces a hardship, such as the loss of wealth, children or worldly provisions, Allah the Almighty is the only one Who can ease their suffering.

When a believer shows patience and forbearance and turns to Allah for assistance, it is He who can give him comfort and grant him salvation from such hardship. Thus, we should strive towards Allah at all times and He will help us immensely.

Questions:

1. How does God help a believer who strives towards Him?
2. At what times should we strive towards Allah?

THE MAGNIFICENCE OF
AYATUL KURSI

Ubayy ibn Ka'ab[ra] relates, 'The Holy Prophet[sas] asked me, "Abu Mundhir, do you know which verse of the Book of Allah is the grandest?" I answered, "The verse of the *Kursi* (2:256)." He poked me in the chest and said, "Felicitations on your knowledge, Abu Mundhir"' (*Muslim*).

اَللّٰهُ لَاۤ اِلٰهَ اِلَّا هُوَ ۚ اَلْحَیُّ الْقَیُّوْمُ ۚ لَا تَاْخُذُهٗ سِنَةٌ وَّ لَا نَوْمٌ ؕ لَهٗ مَا فِی السَّمٰوٰتِ وَ مَا فِی الْاَرْضِ ؕ مَنْ ذَا الَّذِیْ یَشْفَعُ عِنْدَهٗۤ اِلَّا بِاِذْنِهٖ ؕ یَعْلَمُ مَا بَیْنَ اَیْدِیْهِمْ وَ مَا خَلْفَهُمْ ۚ وَ لَا یُحِیْطُوْنَ بِشَیْءٍ مِّنْ عِلْمِهٖۤ اِلَّا بِمَا شَآءَ ۚ وَسِعَ کُرْسِیُّهُ السَّمٰوٰتِ وَ الْاَرْضَ ۚ وَ لَا یَئُوْدُهٗ حِفْظُهُمَا ۚ وَهُوَ الْعَلِیُّ الْعَظِیْمُ

Allah — there is no God but He, the Living, the Self-Subsisting and All-Sustaining.

Slumber seizes Him not, nor sleep. To Him belongs whatsoever is in the heavens and whatsoever is in the earth. Who is he that will intercede with Him except by His permission? He knows what is before them and what is behind them; and they encompass nothing of His knowledge except what He pleases. His knowledge extends over the heavens and the earth; and the care of them burdens Him not; and He is the High, the Great. (Quran, 2:256)

Everything has a pinnacle. *Surah Al-Baqarah* is the pinnacle of the Quran and it has a verse which is the chief of all verses; this is the *Ayatul Kursi*. *Ayatul Kursi* is the most majestic verse of the Quran because it cites divine attributes. The grandeur of God is beyond our comprehension. However, by reflecting on this verse, we can get a better understanding of God's magnificence as well as derive beneficence from His attributes.

Some people spend an entire day sitting in front of a single painting in an art gallery, trying to understand the message that the picture is trying to convey. What one can understand by carrying out an in-depth study of the painting, cannot be understood by just casting a cursory glance over it. Similarly, by studying *Ayatul Kursi* in depth, we can benefit from obtaining a better understanding of the exalted status of God, than if we just briefly glance over it.

Questions:

1. Why is *Ayatul Kursi* the grandest verse of the Quran?
2. What can we gain from studying this verse in detail?

MERITS OF WORSHIP

Abu Hurairah[ra] relates that the Holy Prophet[sas] said, 'If people realized the beneficence of calling the *Azan* and standing in the first row for prayer and they could secure these privileges only through drawing lots they would draw lots for them; and if they knew the merit of coming early to prayer they would vie with each other in their hastening to it; and if they appreciated the value of the dawn and evening prayers they would come to them even if they had to crawl on all fours' (*Bukhari* and *Muslim*).

Worship brings us closer to God; which is the ultimate object of our life. God Almighty does not benefit from our worship, but we benefit from it as it is our opportunity to fulfill our purpose in life. We should take every opportunity to exceed in our worship of God. Thauban[ra] relates that he heard the Holy Prophet[sas] say, 'Multiply your prostrations. Every prostration before Allah will raise your status one degree and will remove one of your sins' (*Muslim*). When we enter a state of absolute humility and engage in sincere worship, a pleasure, a light, and comfort are attained. When the soul of a person is completely humbled, he becomes entirely devoted to God and breaks every tie with whatever exists besides Allah. It is only sincere worship which enables us to reach this spiritual apex.

The Holy Prophet[sas] said, 'Tell me if one of you had a stream running at his door and he should take a bath in it five times every day, would any dirt be left upon him?' He was answered, 'No dirt would be left on him.' The Holy Prophet[sas] stated, 'This is the case of the five prayers. Allah wipes out all faults in consequence of them' (*Bukhari* and *Muslim*). Thus, worship removes our sins. It leaves in its place a light and an illumination, and we become the recipient of God's blessings and love. There is no greater reward for a person than to experience true love for God. This is the ultimate pleasure of all.

Questions:

1. What is the object of man's life?
2. How does a believer benefit from engaging in sincere worship?

COVER THE FAULTS OF OTHERS

Abu Hurairah[ra] relates that Prophet Muhammad[sas] said, 'Allah will cover up the faults on the Day of Judgment of him who covers up the faults of another in this world' (*Muslim*).

God covers up a believer with numerous covers. Each time a believer sins, a cover is torn until there remains no cover. This is when God says to His angels to cover His servant with their wings. If the believer repents upon being covered by the angels, Allah restores the covers; in fact, He restores them nine-fold. However, if the believer does not repent, God tells the angels to abandon him.

One of the attributes of Allah is that He is *Sattar*;

that is, He forgives and covers weaknesses. The Holy Prophet[sas] said that in the Hereafter, God, sheltering man with his mercy, will ask him if he did such and such deed. Man will confess that yes, he did. God will say I covered your fault on that day and I cover your fault again. God covers up our weaknesses and failings and likes us to cover up the flaws and mistakes of others.

We should reflect on the attributes of Allah and strive to adopt them on a human level. This does not mean that we should support failings, instead, we should not circulate them or backbite. It is better to counsel and pray for someone when one notices a weakness or short-coming in them. But exposing the weakness to others is a form of back-biting, it can create disorder in society and it is displeasing to Allah. A true believer concerns himself with his own weaknesses and how to overcome them, rather than analyzing the faults of others and highlighting them.

Questions:

1. What can we do when we notice a shortcoming in someone else?

2. Instead of analyzing the weaknesses of others, what should we be doing?

CHOICE OF SPOUSE

The Holy Prophet[sas] said that 'In marrying a woman, a man's choice of a spouse is determined by the consideration of her wealth, her family, her physical beauty and her religious piety, but you should make your life happy, prosperous and successful by choosing a spouse on account of her religious piety, otherwise your hands will ever remain in dust' (*Bukhari*).

The Holy Prophet[sas] counseled his followers that they should select their spouse based on a woman's level of piety. He said this was so that one's family life would be happy and full of bliss. Wealth and beauty can be temporary, one who based their marriage on these qualities would enjoy a brief and superficially pleasant break but would not have true and abiding felicity. What establishes a happy home life are piety and moral qualities. These solid qualities should be preferred over temporary pleasures. A pious wife is also the provision for the well-being of the next generation. The lasting good effect that a virtuous and good-natured wife has on children is a permanent gift. Any sensible person should desire, for his comfort and the welfare of his offspring, that he is attached to a pious wife. The early upbringing of children is in the hands of the mother, if, therefore, the mother is devout and of high character, the children, would naturally be well-grounded in good morals.

The above hadith, however, does not mean that in selecting a spouse all other considerations should be ignored entirely. All that it means is that piety and moral excellence should be preferred. The Holy Prophet[sas] did also say that a man may look at his wife-to-be so that after marriage he is not unhappy on account of her appearance.

Questions:

1. Why did the Holy Prophet[sas] recommend a man to choose his spouse based on her religious piety?

2. What issues can arise by selecting a wife based only on her other merits?

CONSIDERATION TOWARDS MINORITIES

Anas bin Maalik[ra] narrates that, a dweller of the desert who had recently accepted Islam was sitting in the company of the Holy Prophet[sas] in the mosque. The Bedouin got up and walked away a few paces and sat down in a corner of the mosque to pass water. Some of the companions of the Prophet[sas] immediately got up to stop him from doing so. But the Prophet[sas] restrained them, pointing out that any interference with the man was bound to cause inconvenience to him and might cause him injury. He told his companions to let the man be and to clean the spot later (*Muslim*).

Prophet Muhammad[sas] was particularly considerate of those who, from lack of cultural training, did not know how to comport themselves well in public. He did not seek to embarrass anyone or reprimand them for something they did not know. On the contrary, he displayed an excellent example of how to regard the tender sensitivities of the disadvantaged and frail members of society. Once the Holy Prophet[sas] was engaged in conversation with some Quraish chiefs when Abd Allah Ibn Umm Maktum, a blind man came up to the Prophet[sas] and started to interrupt the conversation. The Prophet[sas] did not like this interference, but his only response was to turn away from Abd Allah (an act he could not see). This incident shows that the Prophet[sas] was careful not to reproach or rebuke Abd Allah, and thus injure his self-respect.

The Holy Prophet[sas] was friendly with slaves, unlike other people who paid them no attention. Bilal[ra], an African slave who converted to Islam, was assigned by the Prophet[sas] as the *Muezzin* (the one who makes the call to prayer). When the Medinites laughed at Bilal's[ra] pronunciation of Arabic words, the Prophet[sas] rebuked them and told them how dear Bilal[ra] was to God because he had endured immense torture from the Meccans when he converted to Islam, but had stayed firm in his faith.

Safiyah[ra], one of the wives of Prophet Muhammad[sas], often received a discriminatory treatment from the Holy Prophet's[sas] other wives because of her Jewish origin. Once Aisha[ra] and Zainab[ra] teased Safiyah[ra] regarding their ethnic superiority by saying that they were not only the Prophet's[sas] wives but were also related to him. When Safiyah[ra] complained about this to the Holy Prophet[sas], he said, 'Safiyah, why didn't you reply saying that your father was Aaron, your Uncle was Moses, and your husband is Muhammad; so how can they be superior to you?' (*Al Tirmidhi*).

At such occasions, the Holy Prophet[sas] did not stay

quiet and let such comments go, because these situations required rectification. The Holy Prophet[sas] used these instances as teaching moments for his followers. He spoke up against those who teased other believers for being different from them. Yet he never reproached those in the wrong more harshly than necessary.

Questions:

1. How did the Prophet[sas] view people of other diversities?
2. How did he deal with people who rebuked those of other diversities?

SELF-CONTROL

Abu Hurairah[ra] **relates that the Holy Prophet**[sas] **said, 'The strong one is not he who knocks out others in wrestling, the strong one is he who keeps control over himself when he is roused'** (***Bukhari*** **and** ***Muslim***).

This hadith teaches us to raise our moral standards and not get caught up in trivial matters. Believers should set a model of humility. It is human nature to feel anger at times, but God has commanded true believers to suppress their anger, treat others with courtesy, reform themselves and try and pay the dues of humankind.

On returning from a battle, the Holy Prophet[sas] once said to his followers that they were returning from the 'lesser jihad' to the 'greater jihad.' He meant that the physical struggles the companions had endured on the battlefield against their human enemies would be less than the moral and spiritual struggles they would fight against their own self. Thus the 'greater jihad' is overcoming one's weaknesses and natural propensity to sin. This can be done by exercising self-control and working on self-reformation.

The beauty of Islam lies in exercising high morals, controlling any form of anger and promoting forgiveness. One who is dignified and humble always avoids quarrels, seeks reconciliation and is courteous to others. This helps produce more peaceful and loving societies.

Questions:

1. Why should we suppress our anger?
2. What is the 'greater jihad'?

ETIQUETTES OF EATING

Umar ibn Abi Salamah[ra] relates, 'I was a boy under the care of the Holy Prophet[sas], and my hand would wander around the bowl when eating. He directed me, "Pronounce the name of Allah, eat with thy right hand and from whatever is in front of thee." This became my way of eating thereafter' (*Bukhari* and *Muslim*).

Eating is a necessity. We need to eat regularly to survive and to have good health. Islam recognizes that a person's eating habits also have a direct impact on his morals and values. For example, exercising self-control in our eating habits translates into more self-control in our other actions too. And eating clean food with clean hands, helps us develop the habit of cleanliness in our other daily activities also.

Aisha[ra] relates that the Holy Prophet[sas] said, 'When any of you begins to eat he should pronounce the name of Allah, the Exalted. If he forgets to do it in the beginning, he should say, "In the name of Allah, first and last"' (*Al-Tirmidhi* and *Abu Dawud*). Our hands should be clean when we eat food, and we should eat with the right hand. Prophet Muhammad[sas] said that 'Blessing descends in the middle of the food, so you should start eating from what is in front of you and do not eat from its middle' (*Al-Tirmidhi* and *Abu Dawud*). He also stressed the importance of finishing all food on a plate, 'Wipe clean the vessel, as you do not know which part of your food is blessed' (*Muslim*). Mu'az ibn Anas[ra] relates that the Holy Prophet[sas] said, 'He who eats a meal and says at the end, "All praise is due to Allah, Who has given me this to eat and provided it for me without any effort on my part or any power," will have all his preceding sins forgiven' (*Al-Tirmidhi*).

Questions:

1. Why should you eat food that is at the front of your plate first?

2. What are some of the other etiquettes of eating in Islam?

PRAYER ON BEHALF OF A BROTHER IN HIS ABSENCE

Abu Darda^{ra} relates that Prophet Muhammad^{sas} often said, 'A Muslim's prayer on behalf of his brother in his absence is responded to. An angel so appointed stands near him and each time he prays for his brother for some good the appointed angel says, "Amen, and may you have the like of it"' (*Muslim*).

To show concern and consideration for others is a virtue. The Holy Prophet^{sas} took every opportunity to highlight the importance of caring for others and building a true bond of brotherhood with other believers. He taught that a true Muslim, loves for his brother what he loves for himself; he forgives their faults and overlooks their weaknesses; he is gentle, kind and humble towards them; he safeguards their reputation, wealth and honor; he is generous, truthful and trustworthy towards them; and he prays for them. And when a believer prays for someone else, God is pleased with him for being concerned about others. Not only is his prayer for his brother accepted, but also God rewards him with the same.

Questions:

1. Why is God pleased with one who prays for his brother?
2. How does a true Muslim treat his brother?

CONTROL ONE'S TONGUE

Ibne Mas'ud[ra] relates that the Holy Prophet[sas] said, 'A believer does not taunt or curse or abuse or talk indecently' (*Al-Tirmidhi*).

The Holy Prophet[sas] often used to stay silent and did not speak unnecessarily. He said, that one who believes in Allah and the Day of Judgement should say something of virtue and goodness or should stay quiet. There is a saying that the wounds caused by a sword heal but the wounds caused by unkind words never heal. This means that we should be mindful that the words that come out of our mouths can never be taken back and can have a lasting effect.

Before speaking, we should ask ourselves if what we are going to say will please Allah or not. If there is even the slightest doubt that what we are about to say may be unkind, hurtful, disrespectful, egoistic, scornful, untruthful, or unnecessary, then we should refrain from speaking it.

Control of one's tongue also means that we should speak the truth. A man once came to The Holy Prophet[sas] and said that he commits three sins in secret. The Holy Prophet[sas] advised the man to promise always to stay firm on honesty. He said if the man were to follow this advice, all his weak points and failings would be eliminated. The man followed this advice and got rid of all his sins, big and small.

When speaking the truth, one should also be mindful of exercising wisdom. Such wisdom requires that everything is said according to the time and place and appropriateness. It is not essential to say everything that is true. If it is not pertinent and appropriate, it can cause discord and conflict. We should be careful to avoid mischief, overstatement and exaggeration, and unnecessary gossip.

Exercising control of our tongue also enables us to remain humble. When we do not keep watch over what we say, our hidden good deeds turn into boasting and we can be harmed quickly by this. Those who are mindful of the many different ways their tongue can cause them and others damage, and take care of what they say, display the true qualities of a believer.

Questions:

1. What are the different ways in which a person causes harm with their tongue?
2. How can we exercise wisdom when speaking the truth?

MERITS OF RECITING
SURAH AL-IKHLAS

The Holy Prophet[sas] inquired from his companions, 'Would any of you find it burdensome to recite one-third of the Quran in the course of a night?' They considered it difficult and said, 'Which of us would have the strength to do that, Messenger of Allah?' He said, '*Surah Al-Ikhlas* is one-third of the Quran' (*Bukhari*).

بِسْمِ اللّٰهِ الرَّحْمٰنِ الرَّحِيْمِ ۝ قُلْ هُوَ اللّٰهُ اَحَدٌ ۝ اَللّٰهُ الصَّمَدُ ۝ لَمْ يَلِدْ ۙ وَ لَمْ يُوْلَدْ ۝ وَ لَمْ يَكُنْ لَّهٗ كُفُوًا اَحَدٌ ۝

In the name of Allah, the Gracious, the Merciful. Say, 'He is Allah, the One; Allah, the Independent and Besought of all. He begets not, nor is He begotten; And there is none like unto Him.' (Quran, 112:1-5)

While every word of the Quran is important in itself, some parts of the Quran hold more significance and grandeur than others. *Surah Al-Ikhlas* is one of the chapters of the Holy Quran which holds the highest of importance in Islam. That is because its subject matter, the Oneness of God, is the fundamental topic of the Holy Quran. This topic is addressed in many chapters of the Quran; however, this short chapter is based solely on this topic and discusses it in a comprehensive and continuous flow.

Anas[ra] relates that the Holy Prophet[sas] said, 'When you recite *Surah Al-Fatihah* and *Surah Al-Ikhlas* upon lying on your bed, you will be safeguarded and should become fearless of everything except death' (*Tafseer Mazhari*). Prophet Muhammad[sas] also encouraged the recitation of *Surah Al-Ikhlas* when someone is on his deathbed as it increases the presence of angels.

There is another hadith about a companion who kept on reciting *Surah Al-Ikhlas* in every *rakah* of *salaat*. The Holy Prophet^sas asked the man why he kept on reciting it in every *rakah*. He replied, 'Because it contains the attributes of the Most Compassionate and I love reading it.' The Holy Prophet^sas then informed the companion that Allah loves him (*Al-Tirmidhi*).

All these hadith demonstrate to us the importance of *Surah Al-Ikhlas* for Muslims and the virtues of reciting it. *Surah Al-Ikhlas* reinforces our belief that God is One, and that God is independent of time and place. And because we believe in Allah Almighty, we do not need help from anyone else. Reflection on the beauty of the Oneness of God as outlined in this Surah will enable us to carry out our worship more purely with a more profound attachment to God.

Questions:

1. What is the significance of reciting *Surah Al-Ikhlas*?

2. In what situations, in particular, should *Surah Al-Ikhlas* be recited?

GIVE CHARITY IN SECRET

Abu Hurairah[ra] narrates that the Holy Prophet[sas] said, 'There are seven whom Allah will shade on the Day of Judgement...[Of these, the sixth is] a man who gives alms with his right hand but conceals it from his left' (*Bukhari* and *Muslim*).

Acts of charity are deemed to be one of the most favorable acts in Islam. There are several hadith and verses in the Holy Quran which tell us that giving charity is a righteous and great act in the eyes of God. The giving of charity provides for those in poverty and is also a means by which the wealthy may achieve nearness to Allah. Even those who have very little are encouraged to give charity, be it food, clothes or labor. The Holy Prophet[sas] mentioned time and time again that the act of charity is commendable and should be performed on a regular basis.

There are two ways to give charity; you can either give charity openly and overtly, or you can give it discretely. The latter carries more reward. A man who gives charity and hides it, so that his left hand does not know what his right hand gives, is a person who cares more about helping other people with good deeds than what other people think of his good deeds. His intentions are concerned solely with helping the needy and pleasing God than with impressing others. However, in some situations, public displays of charitable donations are preferred because they encourage others to follow suit.

Questions:

1. Why is giving charity in secret preferred over giving charity publicly?

2. In what situations might public displays of charitable donations be preferred?

MORAL TRAINING OF CHILDREN

The Holy Prophet^{sas} said, 'The best gift a parent can give their children is their correct training' (*Al-Tirmidhi*).

The Quran (3:36) gives guidelines for the moral training of children from even before their birth and the Holy Prophet^{sas} said that children should be taught good manners from their childhood. It is the duty of every parent to teach their children about faith and not only be occupied in the pursuit of their secular education and worldly endeavors. This is to ensure that our children live a righteous life and our future generations are also dedicated to God's cause. The Holy Prophet^{sas} informed that three prayers are accepted by God without any doubt: the prayer of a father for his children, the prayer of a person on a journey and the prayer of a person who is persecuted (*Ibne Majah*). Prayers, combined with a good moral upbringing, are the key to a pious progeny.

The Holy Prophet^{sas} said, 'Each of you is a shepherd and each of you is responsible for his flock. The ruler over the people is a shepherd and he is responsible for his flock. A man is the shepherd of his family and he is responsible for his flock. A woman is the shepherd of her husband's household and she is responsible for her flock' (*Bukhari* and *Muslim*). Thus, parents have been given the responsibility of raising their children well. And just as sheep follow their shepherd, so do children look to the example of their parents and model that same behavior. So for the proper upbringing of their children, parents need to be an example of piety and righteousness for their children.

The Holy Prophet^{sas} has instructed that parents should not hurt the feelings of their children. They should be kind to them. They should treat all their children equally and be careful to fulfill the promises they make with their children. Once the Holy Prophet's^sas grandsons came to see him. He picked them up and kissed them and cuddled them affectionately. A Bedouin who was watching him said, 'O Messenger of Allah, we have never shown affection to our children as you have shown.' The Prophet^sas replied, 'If you are deprived of love and mercy for your children, what can I do?' (*Bukhari*).

The Holy Prophet^sas emphasized to parents that they should educate their children in the best possible manner and develop in them respect for elders. The Prophet^sas laid great stress on the education of girls. This way, they would become good mothers and bring up their children well. Also, being well-educated, they would be able to contribute more to society.

Questions:

1. Why should believers be concerned about the proper moral upbringing of their children?

2. How can a believer try to give his children a good moral upbringing?

FOCUS ON YOUR HEARTS AND YOUR ACTIONS

The Holy Prophet[sas] said, 'Allah does not see towards your shapes and your wealth, but He sees towards your hearts and your actions' (*Muslim*).

Focusing too much on one's physical appearance or on acquiring wealth leads to self-centeredness and distracts one away from the true worship of God. On the day of judgment, God will not evaluate our physical beauty or our bank balances; instead He will reward us for doing good deeds in this life. A person's wise mind, hard-working hands, and kind heart will serve him well on the Day of Judgment, but the features and fairness of his face or the size of his property will have no benefit for him that day.

The activities of this world and its wealth should only be adopted to the extent that faith remains the ultimate objective. Thus, a believer should seek to improve his thoughts and actions, instead of taking pride in the gifts of physical beauty and worldly goods, as these are things which do not carry forward to the next life.

The Holy Prophet[sas] warned that in the latter days there will be people who will have regard only for appearance and will be opposed to internal improvement. He was asked, why that would be. He answered, because of their desire to please some and out of fear of others.

The above hadith does not mean that a Muslim should not pay any attention to his or her physical appearance. Islam requires believers to be clean and presentable and take good care of their health. These things enable a believer to carry out his faith in a better manner. But we should not be so engrossed in our physical appearance that we become self-centered or arrogant as a result of it.

Questions:

1. What qualities should a believer seek to improve?

2. Why does Islam encourage people not to focus too much attention on wealth and physical beauty?

MODESTY AND PURDAH

Abdullah ibn Abbas[ra] narrates, 'Al-Fadl bin Abbas[ra] rode behind Allah's Messenger[sas] as his companion rider on the back portion of his camel on the day of Nahr and Al-Fadl was a handsome man. The Prophet[sas] stopped to give the people verdicts regarding their matters. In the meantime, a beautiful woman from the tribe of Khatham came, asking the verdict of Allah's Messenger. Al-Fadl started looking at her as her beauty attracted him. The Prophet[sas] looked behind while Al-Fadl was looking at her; so, the Prophet[sas] held out his hand backward and caught the chin of Al-Fadl and turned his face to the other side so that he should not gaze at her' (*Bukahri*).

In Islam, women are commanded to observe the veil, that is, to conceal their physical beauty from men. However, men are instructed in the first instance to restrain their looks at women. We see in this example that while the Prophet[sas] attended to the woman's question, he was careful about not looking at her. He did not ask the woman to cover her face but made it his responsibility to look elsewhere. He also turned the face of his cousin to the side who was staring at the woman's beautiful face. This shows that the Prophet[sas] acted himself, and made other men also act on Allah's orders to lower their gazes.

Modest and chaste behavior is fundamental to the teachings of Islam so that people can live a righteous life and for the good of all society. Islam greatly emphasizes the importance of safeguarding and protecting one's chastity. The intermingling of the sexes is not permitted in Islam so that situations which cannot be controlled afterward, are not allowed to develop in the first place.

Questions:

1. Is purdah only the responsibility of women?

2. Why does Islam enjoin modest and chaste behavior?

GRATEFULNESS TO GOD

Prophet Muhammad[sas] spent long hours in prayers at night. He stood so long in the course of these prayers that sometimes his feet became swollen. On one occasion, Aisha[ra] inquired after the Holy Prophet[sas], 'Messenger of Allah, why do you stand so long in prayer when Allah has suppressed in you, in the past, and for the future, all inclination towards sin?' He answered, 'Aisha, God has been so profuse in bestowing His bounties upon me that it behooves me to be the most grateful servant of Allah' (*Bukhari* and *Muslim*).

Remembrance of Allah is the best way to show sincere gratitude to God, for His numberless bounties. The Holy

Prophet^{sas} spent a significant portion of his time during the day and the night in the worship and praise of God. God's blessings on us are endless and we should express our gratefulness for all He has given us. Also, God has promised the one who displays the quality of gratitude, that He will gift him with more blessings (Quran, 14:8).

The Holy Prophet^{sas} was always grateful to Allah Almighty for His blessings. He was always on the lookout for opportunities to be thankful to Allah and would never miss out on any such opportunity where he could express his utmost gratitude to Him. The Holy Prophet^{sas} was grateful to Allah for even the smallest of things. He praised the Lord when it rained. He praised Him after a meal. He would read a prayer when wearing a new piece of clothing, before going to bed and on waking up, and before going to the bathroom. No aspect of life was neglected by the Holy Prophet^{sas} concerning gratitude towards Allah.

The Holy Prophet^{sas} said that one who is not grateful and does not appreciate little things is also not thankful for larger blessings. He taught his followers to be aware of those who are in a less fortunate position than them and not to focus on those better off than them and said that this too is an expression of gratefulness. He also said that one who is not grateful to people is not thankful to Allah either.

Some people turn towards God only in times of adversity, but a true believer remembers God at all times. A true believer is one that during comfort, displays thankfulness and during trials, displays patience.

Questions:

1. At what times should we be grateful to God?
2. Why should we look to those who are less fortunate than ourselves?

RICH AND POOR EAT TOGETHER

Abu Hurairah[ra] reports that the Holy Prophet[sas] said that 'The worst feast is the one to which the wealthy have been invited and from which the poor have been left out. And whoso declined an invitation (to a meal), he verily sinned against God and disobeyed His Prophet' (*Muslim*).

The Holy Prophet[sas] commanded that when the rich arrange a feast, they must invite the poor also, and when asked to a meal by the poor, the rich should not decline their invitation. This Islamic teaching lays the foundation to promote better social interaction among the rich and the poor and help bridge the gap between the two. This way, we can produce more harmonious societies where the rich are sensitive to the needs and feelings of the poor and do not perceive themselves as superior to them.

Prophet Muhammad[sas] did not like that some people ate lavishly while others had no food to eat. Once he was out walking and came across a group of people who were roasting a lamb. They invited him to join them. But he refused as he did not like that there were poor people around who had no food at all and had not been invited to the meal. In another hadith, the Holy Prophet[sas] said, 'If a poor man invited me to a meal of goat's cooked feet, I would accept his invitation' (*Bukhari*).

Questions:

1. Why should the rich accept an invitation from the poor?
2. How can food be used as a way to bridge the gap between the rich and the poor?

SELF-REFLECT

Shaddad ibn Aus[ra] relates that the Holy Prophet[sas] said, 'A wise person is one who watches over himself and restrains himself from that which is harmful and strives for that which will benefit him after death, and a foolish one is he who gives rein to his cravings and seeks from Allah the fulfillment of his vain desires' (*Al-Tirmidhi*).

It is a good habit for believers to constantly self-reflect and strive to make good deeds a permanent part of their lives. We should always remember that God knows our intentions and sees all of our actions. As a believer, we should continuously self-reflect to identify our shortcomings so that we can work on eradicating them. We should look out for those deeds that are based on righteousness and protect ourselves from those actions that take us away from righteousness. Satan is always trying to tempt one by presenting sin in a beautiful form so that one would start following it. God thus warns us not to go near such things. Reading the five daily prayers protects a believer from indecency. Also, we should have knowledge of, and follow the 700 commandments given by God in the Holy Quran.

In particular, God has appointed the month of Ramadan for Muslims to self-reflect and bring about a positive change in themselves. Ramadan is an opportunity for Muslims to engage further in good deeds and draw closer to God and make these virtues a permanent part of their lives.

God states that one who is firm on righteousness should be cautious and seek God's help before doing anything. Do not be attracted by something that has apparent beauty. Where there is the slightest indication of doubt, thoroughly explore it. Seek God's help and guidance to protect yourself from adverse consequences.

Questions:

1. What is the difference between a wise person and a foolish person?
2. How can we protect ourselves from indecencies?

THE EFFECTS OF ABLUTION

Abu Hurairahra **relates that he heard the Holy Prophet**sas **say, 'My people will be called on the Day of Judgement bright-faced and white-limbed, from the effects of their ablutions; then whoever of you can afford to extend his brightness, let him do so'** (***Bukhari*** **and** ***Muslim***).

Ablution helps us to cleanse ourselves physically, as well as spiritually. The fact that a Muslim performs ablution five times a day ensures that parts of the body that get dirty during the day are physically cleaned and stay pure throughout the day. When our bodies are clean on the outside, then we can attain inner purification also. A pure mind in a pure body is a Muslim's goal.

The Holy Prophetsas said, 'When a Muslim, or a

believer, washes his face (in the course of ablution), every sin which he committed with his eyes, will be washed away from his face with water; when he washes his hands, every sin which is committed by his hands will be effaced from his hands with the water, and when he washes his feet, every sin his feet committed will be washed away with the water; until he finally emerges cleansed of all his sins' (*Muslim*).

The Prophet^{sas} once asked Bilal^{ra}, 'What great virtue do you possess, Bilal? For I have seen you ahead of me in paradise and I could hear your footsteps wherever I went during the *Miraj*.' Bilal^{ra} replied humbly, 'O, Messenger of Allah, I have no virtue except that throughout my life I have tried not to sin, and if ever I do any wrong, at once I perform ablution and say two *Rakahs* of voluntary prayers and implore God for His forgiveness and mercy. And I always try to retain my ablution. Whenever the state of ablution lapses I immediately regain it by performing ablution and offering two *Rakahs* of prayer. O

Prophet of Allah, I do not possess anything besides this.' The Prophet^{sas} replied, 'O Bilal, this is the cause of your good fortune and blessings' (*Muslim*).

All the things believers are required to do are ordained to purify their hearts. Since 'The key to Paradise is *salaat*, and the key to *salaat* is cleanliness,' performing ablution draws us closer to God (*Al-Tirmidhi*). On the Day of Resurrection, a light will shine through the hands and feet of believers because of their habit of performing ablution. This means that those who regularly performed ablution will be distinguished from others by their virtue of keeping themselves pure and clean.

Questions:

1. What are the physical effects of performing ablution?
2. What are the spiritual effects of performing ablution?

KEEP GOOD COMPANY

Abu Musa Ash'ari[ra] relates, the Holy Prophet[sas] said, 'A man who keeps company with virtuous people is like a person who carries about musk with him. If he partakes of it, he derives benefit from it; if he sells it, he makes a profit out of it, and if he merely keeps it, he enjoys its perfume. A man who keeps company with evil persons is like one who blows into a charcoal furnace; all that he can expect is that a spark may alight upon his clothes and set them on fire or that the gas emitted by the charcoal may upset his brain' (*Bukhari* and *Muslim*).

A man's character is affected by the company he keeps. Befriending people of high morals helps us improve our own morals too. When we see good behavior, we have the opportunity to develop a love for it and adopt its practice also. For instance, if everyone around us is punctual and regular in observing prayers, then we are likely to engage in this practice too. It is human nature to pick up the habits of the people that surround us that is why it is crucial that we surround ourselves with righteous people. God is further pleased with those people who are the source of good and inspire others to do good. Their reward is even greater. We should be vigilant about making good friends and acquiring good habits from them.

Keeping bad company can lead one to immorality and is a form of self-destruction. Sometimes people do not realize they are doing something wrong because everyone around them is doing the same. For example, in societies where lying is common practice, people soon do not feel any remorse at lying. Therefore, one should educate oneself on the true teachings of Islam so that we can always be conscientious of what is right and what is wrong and act accordingly.

Questions:

1. What are the benefits of keeping good company?
2. How can we protect ourselves from committing sins that are standard practice in our societies?

ARRIVE EARLY FOR FRIDAY PRAYERS

Abu Hurairah[ra] relates that Prophet Muhammad[sas] said that, 'On Friday, angels stand by the door of the mosque and note down the example of he who arrives first to the mosque as equivalent to one who had sacrificed a camel for winning Allah's pleasure, and he who arrives to the mosque after him, as equivalent to one who had sacrificed a cow, and he who arrives after him, as equivalent to one who had sacrificed a chicken, and he who arrives after him, as equivalent to one who had sacrificed an egg. When the Imam arrives, the angels close their register and crowd in to listen to his sermon' (*Bukhari* and *Muslim*).

This hadith narrates the significance of Friday prayers in Islam. Friday is the most excellent of all days in the sight of God. The Holy Prophet Muhammad[sas] said about the importance of Friday, 'It is the day Adam was born, it is the day he was sent down to earth, it is the day he passed away, it is the day during which a moment comes when anything that is asked for, save what is forbidden, will be granted and it is the day when the Day of Judgement will come to pass' (*Muslim*).

On Fridays, Muslims are required to abandon all worldly affairs and come to the mosque punctually and join in the special blessings of this day. As the above hadith states, Allah is most pleased with those people who give priority and show eagerness towards this blessed day and thus arrive punctually for Friday prayers. Prophet Muhammad[sas] stated that Fridays are a weekly Eid for Muslims. Friday is an opportunity for Muslims to spiritually cleanse themselves and become closer to God. The reward for carrying out good deeds is increased manifold on Fridays. Every Friday, the Holy Prophet[sas], used to take a bath, wear clean clothes and wear fragrance before proceeding to the mosque.

Questions:

1. Why is Friday the most important day of the week for Muslims?
2. What should Muslims do on a Friday?

PARADISE FOR THOSE WHO FAST

Saad ibn Sahl[ra] relates that the Holy Prophet[sas] said, 'There is a gate of Paradise called *Rayyan* through which only those will enter on the Day of Judgment who are regular in observing the fast and no one else. A call will go forth, "Where are those who observed the fast regularly?" And they will step forth and no one beside them will enter through that gate. After they have entered, the gate will be closed and no one else will enter thereby' (*Bukhari* and *Muslim*).

The above hadith mentions a gate of paradise, *Rayyan*. This is not a physical gate made of wood or iron at the entrance of Heaven. The word *Rayyan* means the pleasure you get when you quench your thirst or fulfill your desire. This pleasure is doubled, when you keep yourself under control from fulfilling your passion for the sake of some loved one and only with His permission quench your thirst. This is what *Rayyan* is, and fasting is the act which leads to *Rayyan*. Believers refrain from eating and drinking for the sake of God and open their fast only at the time prescribed by God. The pleasure that is felt by believers when they open their fast is *Rayyan*. This pleasure is paradise for a believer and only those who fast can experience this pleasure.

The month of Ramadan provides an opportunity every year for believers to become more righteous. When one fasts with sincerity, being righteous will bring him or her in the refuge of Allah the Almighty. The Holy Prophet[sas] said that whoever observes fasting during Ramadan in a state of faith and while self-evaluating, his previous sins will be forgiven and if believers knew what the excellences of Ramadan are, they would have wished that the entire year was Ramadan. Other hadith relate that during Ramadan God opens the doors to Paradise and shuts the doors leading to Hell and restrains Satan. During Ramadan, believers should make every effort to enter Paradise through all the doors that are open. That is, we should try to carry out those deeds which are pleasing to God. Ramadan is a special month for the acceptance of prayer and to become closer to God. When one finds God, all of one's other wishes and desires are taken care of.

Questions:

1. What does the word '*Rayyan*' mean?
2. What is the purpose of the month of Ramadan?

RESTORE THE TIES OF KINSHIP

Abu Hurairah[ra] relates that a man said to the Holy Prophet[sas] 'My relatives are such that I join the ties of kinship with them and they cut them asunder, and I am benevolent towards them and they ill-treat me, and I forbear, and they are churlish.' He said, 'If you are as you have said, you are feeding them hot ash, and so long as you continue as you are, you will always have a helper from Allah against them' (*Muslim*).

The Holy Prophet[sas] established family peace by identifying balanced rights and obligations of all its members – the parents, the spouses, the children, and the relatives. He was the first to establish the dignity and rights of women. He outlined the rights of orphans, the divorced and the widowed. To establish family peace, he preached to be kind, express love, control anger, stop back-biting, forgive faults, etc.

One should maintain an excellent relationship with one's relatives for one's own moral development. Even if the other party ill-treats you, you must fulfill your obligation towards them for the sake of God. A true believer can overlook the faults of others, holds no grudges or feelings of superiority and demonstrates kindness and compassion in all situations. A believer is the initiator of peace and is a humble servant of God, always wishing to please Him. The Holy Prophet[sas] said, 'He who severs the ties of kinship will not enter paradise' (*Muslim*). He counseled his followers that Allah will become a friend of those who are good to their relatives. Meanwhile, those relatives who mistreat them will be held accountable for their bad conduct.

Questions:

1. According to the Holy Prophet^{sas}, how should believers treat relatives who mistreat them?

2. What would be the result of doing this?

LOVE NOT LUXURY

When Mu'adh ibn Jabal^{ra} was appointed Governor of Yemen, the Holy Prophet^{sas} said to him, 'Beware of luxury for the true servants of Allah love not luxury' (*Ahmad bin Hanbal*).

The Holy Prophet^{sas} emphasized the virtue of living a simple life. He warned his followers that when they are blessed with worldly provisions, they should not become engrossed in a life of ease and luxury, as they too would perish like the civilizations before them did. He said, 'Cursed is the worshipper of dinars and dirhams and the one lost in the pursuit of this world' (*Bukhari*). He commented that truly rich is a person who has no desire for that which others have.

A righteous person is content with little and is not interested in a life of ease and luxury, whereas a materialistic person is not satisfied until they have the best of everything. The Holy Prophet[sas] said 'I have no connection with this world; my relation with this world is only of a transitory kind like that of a rider who stops by a shady tree while traveling. He rests for a short while in the shade and then takes off' (*Al-Tirmidhi*).

The Holy Prophet[sas] could have had any and every kind of luxury of this life, but he chose instead to live a life of austerity. His clothes were simple. His food was simple. His house and furniture were simple. He slept on a rough mattress and reclined on a coarse mat which left impressions on his skin. When he was asked why he did not use soft mattresses and couches like the rulers of other countries, he replied, that they had chosen this world, whereas he had chosen the next.

Staying away from an extravagant lifestyle also brings one closer to poor people. Those who maintain a high standard of living often look down upon the poor and are less likely to mix with them, causing divisions in society. By choosing the path of simplicity, one can distance themselves from a material life and enhance their soul for its true purpose.

Questions:

1. Why did the Holy Prophet^{sas} not adopt a life of ease and luxury?
2. What is the difference between a materialistic person and a righteous person?

TAKE CARE OF YOUR
NEIGHBORS

Abu Dharr[ra] relates that Prophet Muhammad[sas] said, 'Abu Dharr, when you prepare broth, put plenty of water in it and take care of your neighbors' (*Muslim*).

The Holy Quran (4:37) says that neighbors should be treated not only with justice but also with kindness. Prophet Muhammad[sas] greatly emphasized kindness towards neighbors and keeping good relations with them. He used to say that the Angel Gabriel had stressed consideration towards one's neighbors so often that he began to think that a neighbor would perhaps be included among the prescribed heirs. Whenever any special food was prepared in his house, he used to suggest that a portion of it should be sent as a gift to his neighbors. Gifts of food and other items were often sent from his house to his neighbor's house. He also taught his followers, to adopt a habit of sharing food with their neighbors. Broth was a typical and favorite dish of the Arabs, that is why he counseled his followers to share this dish with their neighbors.

The Holy Prophet[sas] taught his followers to help their neighbor if they seek help, give them a loan if they ask for a loan; give them relief if they are needy; nurse them if they fall ill; follow their coffin if they die; rejoice with them if they meet any good; sympathise with them if any calamity befalls them; raise not your building so as to deprive them of air without their permission; and harass them not. Islam sets the guidelines to bind humanity into one, single family based on love, respect and care towards each other, creating an environment of peace, well-being, and prosperity for all.

Note: The concept of 'neighborhood' in Islam is a

broad concept, which covers all possible neighborly situations and is not confined to the ordinary concept of door-to-door neighbors. It can be applied to one's local community, workplace, and even neighboring countries, depending on the situation.

Questions:

1. To which groups of people can the word 'neighbor' in Islam refer?
2. Why did the Prophet Muhammad[sas] think that neighbors might be included among the prescribed heirs in Islam?

ENTER THE MOSQUE WITH A CLEAN BREATH

Jabir^{ra} relates that the Holy Prophet^{sas} said, 'He who has eaten garlic or onions, or any other malodorous herb should not approach our mosque for angels also suffer from that which causes suffering to humans' (*Muslim*).

Cleanliness is fundamental to the Islamic faith. The Holy Prophet^{sas} said that 'Cleanliness is half of faith' (*Muslim*). That is because the condition of the body affects the mind. When we are physically clean, then we are more likely to act and think cleanly too. The Holy Prophet^{sas} said when you go to visit someone, tidy up your clothes and your mouths because Allah does not like dirt and untidiness.

Prophet Muhammad^{sas} always washed his hands before and after eating and used to brush his teeth several times a day. He also emphasized the importance of keeping mosques clean and stressed that worshippers should pay extra attention towards their cleanliness when going to the house of God. Muslims are instructed to take a bath before going to Friday prayers and spray themselves with musk. Some foods cause us to have bad breath, so we should be careful not to eat anything malodorous before going to the mosque or take care to clean our mouths appropriately after eating such foods so that our mouths are not left with a bad smell which would be unpleasant to other worshippers.

Questions:

1. In what ways can a Muslim keep himself/herself clean?
2. Why is cleanliness so important in Islam?

AN EXEMPLARY HUSBAND

Once Safiyyah[ra], wife of the Holy Prophet Muhammad[sas] was traveling with the Prophet Muhammad[sas]. She used to enwrap herself in a sheet and sit behind him on the camel's back. Whenever she had to mount the camel, the Holy Prophet Muhammad[sas] offered his knee for her to step on. The camel on which the Holy Prophet[sas] and Safiyyah[ra] were riding, slipped and they both fell. A companion, Abū Talah[ra], ran towards the Prophet Muhammad[sas] to offer his assistance. But the Prophet[sas] directed him to go to the aid of Safiyyah[ra] first (*Bukhārī*).

The Holy Quran (4:20) tells men to be kind and affectionate to their wives. A man has responsibilities as the guardian of the household and as a husband. If he fulfills these duties, it can establish love and harmony in his home and become a means of peace in the wider society. The Holy Prophet^sas said that a man who puts a morsel of food into his wife's mouth with a desire to earn merit in the sight of God does a deed equal in virtue to giving alms.

Prophet Muhammad^sas was an exemplary husband. He tended to the needs and tender sensitivities of his wives with love and kindness. He told his followers, 'The best of you is one who is best in his treatment of his wife, and I am the best of you in this treatment' (*Al-Tirmidhi*). Prophet Muhammad^sas helped around the house. Aisha^ra relates that he would stitch his own clothes, mend his shoes and repair household items such as the water bucket.

On his last pilgrimage to Mecca, the Holy Prophet^sas told his followers to be kind to women. He said that men should take very good care of their women and provide for all of their necessities and treat them with kindness and courtesy. On another occasion, he warned his followers, 'Beware of the two weak ones – women and orphans. Discharge your duties to them well. Be kind to them and do not ill-treat them' (*An-Nasai*). He also advised that a husband should overlook minor faults in his wife and not make any fuss over such slips on her part. He said, 'No believer should ever bear a grudge against his wife because of an imperfection of hers, for if she has an imperfection, she has some loveable virtues also which please him' (*Muslim*). Good treatment of wives is thus also a sign of the greatness of one's standard of faith.

Questions:

1. What advice did the Holy Prophet[sas] give his followers about how they should treat their wives?
2. Give examples from the life of Prophet Muhammad[sas] that demonstrate that he was an exemplary husband?

SIMPLICITY IN EATING

Miqdad ibn Ma'dikarib[ra] relates that he heard the Holy Prophet[sas] say, 'No man fills a vessel worse than his stomach. A few mouthfuls that would suffice to keep his back upright are enough for a man, but if he must eat more, then he should fill one third with food, one third with drink and leave one third for easy breathing' (*Al-Tirmidhi*).

Moderation and balance are essential aspects of Islam. The Holy Prophet[sas] said, 'Do good deeds properly, sincerely and moderately. Always adopt a middle, moderate, regular course, whereby you will reach your target (of Paradise)' (*Bukhari*). He applied this rule to eating also. He taught his followers not to eat or drink excessively. In today's society, overeating is common practice in developed nations, leading to health issues and fad diets, yet at the same time, in underdeveloped countries, people are dying of starvation.

Prophet Muhammad^sas himself exercised very simple eating habits. It is recorded that he never ate his fill. Aisha^ra narrates, 'We often did not even light the stove for several days. We only ate dates and drank water. Due to our humble circumstances, the members of the household of the Holy Prophet^sas were not able to eat bread for more than three days in a row' (*Bukhari*).

Exercising control in our eating habits helps us to develop self-control in our other habits also. Jabir^ra relates that the Holy Prophet^sas asked for sauce and was told there was nothing but vinegar. He called for it and began to eat his food with it, exclaiming, 'What excellent sauce is vinegar; what excellent sauce is vinegar' (*Muslim*). Prophet Muhammad^sas was grateful for whatever food was available. He never complained about food and he never overindulged in eating. He demonstrated that simple and controlled eating habits translate to more discipline in our other actions also.

Questions:

1. Why did the Prophet Muhammad[sas] teach simplicity in eating?
2. What should we do when we don't like the food that is served to us?

TAKE CARE OF ORPHANS

Sahl ibn Sa'd[ra] reports that 'The Holy Prophet[sas], said, "A person who treats an orphan, boy or girl, with kindness and favor will be with me in Paradise like these two," and the Holy Prophet[sas] indicated to his two joined fingers' (*Bukhari*).

Taking care of orphans is an obligation God has placed on Muslims (Quran, 2:221). Looking after an orphan is not a favor that somebody does for the orphan; rather the upbringing and training of orphans is the responsibility of society. It is the right of orphans to have someone take care of them in place of their parents.

Those entrusted with the care of orphans should be mindful of their education and training. The objective is to bring them up in a manner that they become the best part of society. There should be no differentiation between their academic training and the academic training of one's own children. Orphans should never be made to feel that due to their misfortune they could not fully reach their potential or that if their parents were alive, they would have had a better life.

Whether the care of orphans is undertaken by individuals or on a communal level, their education and training and supervision is the responsibility of those who are in charge of their care. The companions of the Holy Prophet[sas] used to strive with each other to look after orphans for they aspired to have a place next to the Prophet[sas] in paradise as well.

Questions:

1. Is taking care of orphans a favor or an obligation on the part of society?
2. How should orphans be treated?

SEEK KNOWLEDGE AND IMPART IT

Abdullah ibn Mas'ud[ra] **relates that 'Allah's Messenger said to me "The best charity on the part of a Muslim is to acquire knowledge and to impart it to others"' (*Al-Tirmidhi*).**

Man's understanding is limited. However, with God's help and guidance, we can continue to explore and discover more about the mysteries of nature and the universe. The Holy Prophet[sas] enjoined that man should seek knowledge from childhood to old age. The Holy Prophet[sas] compared assemblies where knowledge is sought to being like Gardens of Paradise. However, he also cautioned not to seek knowledge in order to feel superior to another or to use it for self-promotion.

The Holy Prophet[sas] said that it is a fine act of charity when a Muslim seeks knowledge and then teaches it to another Muslim. When people have knowledge of something they should impart it to others.

Allah revealed the perfect Book to the Holy Prophet[sas] complete with knowledge of every possible kind. Thus, the best knowledge is obtained through the study and understanding of the Holy Quran. The study of the Holy Quran provokes understanding of the ways of the world. Human intellect is challenged to investigate and verify its claims. For this reason, the Holy Prophet[sas] commented that 'The best among you is the one who learns the Quran and teaches it to others' (*Bukhari*).

Questions:

1. Which reasons for gaining knowledge did the Holy Prophet[sas] caution his believers against?
2. Why should believers study the Holy Quran?

SPEAK UP AGAINST OPPRESSION

The Holy Prophet[sas] said, 'Go to the aid of your brother, whether he is an oppressor or oppressed.' Someone asked, 'Messenger of Allah, we know how to help one who is oppressed, but how shall we help one who is the oppressor?' He answered, 'Hold his hand so that he stops oppressing' (*Bukhari* and *Muslim*).

Muslims are required to have compassion for anyone who is oppressed and help them win their freedom from oppression, without them even having to ask. We shouldn't just be bystanders or simply express our dislike when somebody commits a wrong against another person. Instead, we should be proactive in counseling the oppressor to end the oppression. The above hadith narrates that a true believer speaks up against what is wrong, even if he might face negative treatment as a result of this. The key to peace is to stop cruelty and oppression, wherever it occurs. When this principle is followed, there will be greater peace in the world.

This hadith does not state that you should take action against your government if you do not agree with its policies. Islam requires you to always obey your ruler. Even if you disapprove of something done by your ruler, you should be patient and pray (unless you are imposed to do something against your religious belief). A ruler will be accountable for the responsibility given to him while the subjects will be accountable for the responsibility laid on them.

The Holy Prophet[sas] said 'If you see something you disapprove of, you should alter it with your hand, if you do not have the strength for this, do so with your speech and if you do not have the strength for this, then do so in your heart, and that is the least of faith' (*Muslim*). The directive to 'alter with your hand' is for rulers, the directive to do so with 'speech' is for *Ulema* (religious scholars) and the directive to dislike something with one's heart is for the believing masses.

Questions:

1. Give some examples of situations which involve oppression.
2. In what circumstances should a Muslim stand up against oppression?

MODERATION IN WORSHIP

Anas[ra] reports, 'Three men came to the houses of the wives of the Prophet[sas] to inquire about the worship of the Prophet[sas]. When they were informed, they considered their worship insignificant and said, "Where are we in comparison with the Prophet while Allah has forgiven his past sins and future sins." One of them said "As for me, I shall offer *salaat* all night long." Another said, "I shall observe fasting continuously and shall not break it." Another said, "I shall abstain from women and shall never marry." The Prophet[sas] came to them and said, "Are you the people who said such and such things? By Allah, I fear Allah more than you do, and I am most obedient and dutiful among you to Him, but still, I observe fast and break it; perform *salaat* and sleep at night and have wives. So whoever turns away from my Sunnah does not belong to me'" (*Bukhari* and *Muslim*).

Prophet Muhammad[sas] constantly encouraged his followers to be moderate in all aspects of life. Some of his followers would occupy themselves so much with prayer and fasting that they would neglect their normal obligations or cause damage to their health. He admonished them for their austerity by stating, 'The religion (of Islam) is easy, and whoever makes the religion a rigor, it will overpower him. So, follow a middle course; if you can't do this, do something near to it and give glad tidings and seek the help of Allah at morn and dusk and some part of the night' (*Bukhari*). Islam teaches its followers not to carry any matter to the extreme. God loves best those acts of worship and piety, which though moderate, are carried out without being felt a burden.

Prophet Muhammad[sas] informed his followers that having performed that which is prescribed, they should pray and fast and worship God while they may do so cheerfully; and stop when their mind or body begins to feel the strain.

Anas[ra] reports that The Prophet[sas] came into the mosque and noticed a rope stretched between two poles. He enquired, 'What is this rope for?' He was told, 'This is Zainab's rope. When during her voluntary prayer, she begins to feel tired, she grasps it for support.' The Prophet[sas] said, 'Untie it. You should perform prayers so long as you feel active. When you feel tired, you should go to sleep' (*Bukhari*). The Prophet[sas] encouraged his companions on many occasions to limit their extra worship so that they could take care of their duties to their families as well as maintain good health. One should be moderate in worship and select such times for optional and voluntary prayers when one feels real pleasure in them.

Questions:

1. In addition to worship of God, what other obligations should worshippers be mindful of?
2. How should one feel when performing optional forms of worship?

REFERENCES

The Holy Quran. Arabic Text with English Translation & Short Commentary. Edited by Farid, M. G. (2002). Surrey: Islam International Publications Limited.

Ahmad, M. B. (2016). *Forty Gems of Beauty* (2nd ed.). Islam International Publications Ltd.

Ahmad, M. B. M. (2003). *Remembrance of Allah* (2nd ed.). Surrey: Islam International Publications Ltd.

Ahmad, M. B. M. (2013). *Life of Muhammad* (6th ed.). Surrey: Islam International Publications Ltd.

Ahmad, M. M. (2003-2018). *Archives of Friday Sermons.* Retrieved from http://www.alislam.org/archives/ky.html

Khan, M, Z. (1980). *Muhammad: Seal of the Prophets.* London: Routledge and Kegan Paul.

Khan, M, Z. (1995). *Wisdom of the Holy Prophet* (4th ed.). Surrey: Islam International Publications Ltd.

Khan, M. Z. (2006). *Gardens of the Righteous* (4th ed.). Surrey: Islam International Publications Ltd.

Orchard, B. A. (1993). *Life Supreme.* Ontario: Islam International Publications Ltd.

Zafar, A. R. (2008). *Etiquette of Life* (1st ed.). Ontario: Islam International Publications Ltd.

ABOUT THE AUTHOR

Bushra Bajwa grew up in Manchester, UK. She has a B.Sc. in International Management from the University of Manchester and a M.Ed. in Student Affairs from Seattle University. She currently lives in Issaquah, Washington with her husband and three young children. Bushra's parents instilled in her from an early age love for, and basic knowledge of the religion of Islam. She wrote this book because of her desire to learn more about the kind, fair and righteous ways of Prophet Muhammad[sas] and to be able to share these ways with her children and the whole world!

Bushra enjoys writing about Islam, interfaith, parenting, nutrition and fitness. She strongly believes that our spiritual journeys need to be supported by healthy bodies. She works as a group fitness instructor and enjoys running 5Ks with her son, horse-back riding with her elder daughter and teaching Spanish to her youngest!

A special thanks to her husband, Hassan Khan, for helping put this book together!

Made in United States
Orlando, FL
16 May 2022

17928245R00086